BE LIKE A BUTTERFLY

11 SIMPLE TOOLS FOR STRESS FREE LIFE

JOLLY JALPA

Made with ♥ on the Notion Press Platform
www.notionpress.com

This Book is dedicated to the most important persons in my life.

My Father for all your love, care, motivation, support and for being idle of my life.The first person
who always inspires me by saying that "You can do it." Always kept me going in life and made
me what I am today.

My Mother for always supporting me in all kinds of decisions and thought me good values in
my life.

My Husband always stood behind me in my all decisions after my Father and motivate
me constantly in my new journey.

My younger Bro, Sister in law, my daughter, and my two Nephews.

And in the last, My Family and My True Friends who always love me and support me.

Contents

Introduction

First of all, congratulation to you for bringing some time for yourself. Yes, if you pick this book in your hand, it means that you want to change something in your life to keep your present- pleasant and your future brighter. And this will happen just because of your one fine decision of reading this book. Time is not a barrier to anything that we want to do in our life. It is just our limiting belief that we have carried with us for a long time.

Each millionaire- billionaire or successful person has the same time, as we are having. Then what is the difference between us and them? This question always put me inside the cyclone of my other so many questions of successful people. Success is not only about wealth or Money. It is about how much you are resourceful to the people around you or the world. How many people are happy with your services and are you satisfied with your service to add value to other's life? Nobody was there to teach our priorities in our childhood. Our parents were also victims of such situations. Even though nobody was there to teach them about priority settings in their life, but still, they always tried their best to teach us.

20th-century children

Like right now we are trying to give our best to the upbringing of our child. And I am sure you all agree with me that these 20th-century kids are much faster than us. We just need to hold their hands properly to show them the right path. So they can find their destiny themselves. Don't be the owner of your child. We are just guardians.

Parenting is not my topic today but a seed of human behaviour, thinking patterns, social activity, beliefs and myths everything is connected to our childhood. See kids are just like a creeper. They will grow in whatever direction you will put them. Only thing is that you cannot force them. Children are a follower of their parents.

When you start doing things for a long time, they will automatically start following you. So start applying those habits in your day-to-day life which u want to see in your child. We could not go outside to change people. We cannot even think about people to change for us. Even though we know this, deep down we always want situations favourable to be in place according to us. And when it does not happen in our favour, our mental health gets disturbed.

We started feeling depressed, stressed, irritated, annoyed, and also feels like every bad thing happened only in our life. Rest all world is so much happy and joyful. Cribbing, complaining and criticising ourselves becomes a routine part of our life. Eventually, it affects our physical health also. As we are thinking to come out of this, instead of that we are deeper down going inside in all these situations. Day by day life becomes more stressful and the whole story of our stressful life begins with this.

About Author

At the age of 34, when I went stuck in this mud I got severe health issues. One day when I came back to my home after picking up my 4-year-old daughter from school, I suddenly become like a statue, just after opening my door lock. I was unable to step forward. My whole spinal cord has become stiff. As I have already spinal cord issue (scoliosis) since my birth, so I become more scared. I could not understand what happened to my spine. I could not move even in any direction. My daughter started crying to see my condition. Standing in the same position, I called up one of my Orthopedic friend about my situation. He advises me to complete bed rest for a minimum of 3 months. I was not allowed to carry 500 gm of weight even. Being a mother of a 4-year-old child it is quite impossible for me to do such kind of rest. My husband used to go office morning from 8 AM to 10 PM. So couldn't ask him also for any kind of help. I was the only person to look out for my whole household responsibility including my daughter.

Life Teaches us

Smile, please. Yes, you are reading right. Smile, please. Don't be emotional. I am not here to tell you my biography or gain sympathy from you. I just want to share, how life teaches us. And if I can bring myself back with 10x time better then you can also do it. Just believe in yourself.

This one incident changes my whole life. I was suggested to do complete bed rest for at least 3 months minimum. Time may be extended. It depends on me only, how fast I recovered. Or you can say depends on my willpower, how I take this challenge? As per the Doctor.

So the first thing was a clear indication that only medicine doesn't work on the human body. There is something else that also takes place in the healing of the human body. Second thing, it is not because of any accident, any people hurt me or any situation that took place because of that I got such kind of situation.

Why

Then why it happened to me? Was my Karma not good? Did I do something wrong to anyone? Why universe gave me this disability in my life? Why I should suffer even though having so much education? Why? Why? Why? So many "Why" started roaming around me.

Let me tell you the truth, I Manifested this situation for myself. I am the only one responsible for my situation Yes. Do not surprise by this sentence. I realised this after taking complete bed rest for around two full months. Before being stuck in this situation, I used to tell everyone for more than 6-8 months that, I want complete bed rest. I am so much tired of these household responsibilities. I have carried out my post-pregnancy body weight of around 82 kg. With scoliosis disorder, 3.9 ft short height, 82 kg body weight, post-pregnancy GYN issues, mood swings, memory loss in small small things, almost lost of my smile, and other so many issues, I was frustrated.

I had given my best to change people around me, tried to make them comfortable according to me, and tried to hold situations according to me and somehow I failed by doing all these things. And when I saw everything is out of control started complaining about my life. And by telling the same sentences again and again somehow the universe listens to me and helps me to fulfil my wish to take rest.

The universe does not understand positive or negative. They just fulfil your wish. Like a twoyear child, who does not know what is good and bad for him. He just does tantrums to fulfil his demand. And we fulfil it, even though we know what is good or bad for him. The same way the universe fulfils every human's wish. Universe never differentiates things by negative or positive. This is called "Law of Attraction".

Every human being uses it knowingly or unknowingly. No one can deny it. People who consciously use it, grow much faster in the right way. People who unconsciously do it, might be go through the wrong path. They might be attracting bad situations or people in their life. That is the only difference between successful people and ordinary people.

Successful people know how to think, talk and take action. They consciously make efforts to change their life. Ordinary people waste their time cribbing complaining and comparison their selves with others and ended up with no results or unwanted results. And again get a chance to complain. And the wheel of life goes on and on.

After taking a rest for so long, at least I realised that I destroyed my life myself. Even though I know about LOA somewhat I did a huge mistake in my life. Also being a Psychology student somewhat I relate to things that are not under my control and emotional distortion of myself.

Decision

So now I decided to wrap up my life in beautiful gift wrap paper filled with all colours of life. I started taking a baby step to "Be like a Butterfly".

I decided to take every action needed for this. I don't have any mentor at that time so started watching Bk Shivani's video on YouTube. Started watching only empowerment and motivational videos on YouTube which can help me to bring out back. I watch Rhonda Byrne's "The Secret" movie again which I already watched about 7-8 years back. I read Rhonda Byrne's "The Magic" book, in which she gives some exercise every day for 30 days continue, which changed my whole perspective on happiness in my life. I am a huge fan of Dr. Joseph Murphy's book – "The Power of Your Subconscious Mind". Which I read when I was doing study in M.A. Psychology. Once again I opened that book and promise myself that from now onwards I will not step out to follow all these rules practically in my life.

And day by day from inside I noticed some changes in myself. But still is not visible outside. With this, I also started meditation, mantra chanting and healing prayer. Which we will discuss in the next chapter in detail. So I am going to share all the secrets that I followed in my life to upgrade myself and change my life from "Depression to Celebration".

It does not happen in one month or two months of the time. It takes about more than a year. But yes I was so much consistent in my efforts and, slowly and gradually I upgrade my frequency. It was also not flawless activity. Circumstances worsen many times but still, I took a stand for a change. I will discuss everything with you in a particular chapter. I try to cover up all major things which impact my life wildly in this book. So if you also relate to such a situation, keep pen and paper with you and be ready to be the "Zero to Hero" Of your own life.

Meditation

"Meditation is the first thing that I have started unknowingly during Covid time to keep away myself from any kind of negativity. Later on, I started enjoying it so much and I increased my meditation time day by day. Right now I am at a stage where 1 hr of meditation feels like 5 min only. I do not feel any kind of distraction."

By reading my experience do not jump to any kind of positive or negative conclusion. But yes, you can start it right now.

How to do meditation?

Meditation is such a simple technique yet very profound. Just seat in a very comfortable position, you can seat on the floor or you can seat in a chair, where ever u feel comfortable in one place, where nobody will disturb you. Wear some comfortable clothes. And close your eyes by focusing on your breath. And just observe your thoughts. Don't push yourself to completely cut off from thoughts. Let the thoughts come in and go. Whenever you realise just divert your focus to your breath.

You can use any kind of music or guided meditation also for this. You can do it at any time, any place. There is no compulsion for meditation to do only in the morning or night. But yes, because these particular times there are fewer chances of disturbance, so you can get more benefit out of it. There is no need for any specialisation or certification for such a profound technique. In the primary stage, you can start with only 5 min, and later on, you can increase your time day by day. It is not that how long time you do meditation will matter. The thing matter is how long you concentrate on your breathing or you focus or aware of your thoughts is matter.

There are so many myths about meditation.
Like

1. It requires a specific time. Meditation should be done in only the early morning.
2. Getting benefits from meditation is time taking process or years of practice are required.
3. Only people who do not want to be socially active, choose such things in their life.
4. One should have a peaceful mind to do meditation properly.
5. I do not have so much time to do meditation. I have other priorities.

Now let me clear all these myths about meditation. So you become relaxed to try it out. Meditation is the easiest and simplest thing but a profound tool for transformation.

Meditation is nowadays so much popular tool for having a stress-free life. No one is denied for that right? But still, I know more than 80% of you accept that they don't have time to do meditation even though they really want to do this practice. Right?

Is it so that mediation is important for living stress-free life only? My answer is: NO. In my case meditation play a tremendous role during the whole journey of my transformation.

What are the major changes I felt in my life after doing Meditation?

1. I started feeling calm and relaxed.
2. I started accepting things, people and situations as they are.
3. My memory power increased.
4. Things become clear to me. I mean, started getting clarity in my life.
5. I started losing weight. Also started getting tips for weight loss out of the box.
6. Started improving my physical and mental health.
7. Becoming more aware of present situations.
8. Getting more energy for doing my work.
9. Started enjoying the household activity.
10. Started getting an intuition for my daily work to be done. And this was a miraculous experience for me.
11. There are some sparkling shining people who started noticing my face after a few months of meditation.
12. I started to accept myself the way I am. Fewer complaints less cribbing after some months.

Other than these there are many more benefits I started gaining only with meditation. Day by day I started to fall in love with this thing. And now whenever I get some time, even though it is 10-15 min, I started seat in one place and close my eyes by concentrating on my breathing only. I am just enjoying this process fully.

We know that our physical body needs rest, so we take good sleep at night, so in the morning again we start a very fresh day. Just like that our mental body (our brain) also needs rest. It is also working since our birth. And adding day by day more information in it, it becomes garbage of information. Giving him rest provide us more clarity, more energy for our work, more concentration, good memory, good health and many more things which we need to continue our daily lives peacefully.

So note down this very important first step to include in your daily life which is meditation. And do remember to share its benefits with me. At the end of the book, I will share my contact details with you for sure.

Now I am ready to share another step that was pinned to me every day. Which I am going to cover in the next chapter - comparison and jealousy.

CHAPTER TWO

Appreciation-No comparison and Jealousy

"This was the most difficult part for me to let go of. I am sure you will agree with me. In today's world, how can someone survive without comparison our self with others? Actually, our day starts with that only."

You all agree with me that this is a very common thing in our daily life to compare ourselves with others. We used to compare our house, our vehicle, our vacation, our food, our clothes, our income, our business, our lifestyle, our ritual, our accessories, and even our kids also, Right?

I was also among these in some areas of my life. I used to compare myself with my other friends on social media and feel jealous so many times by watching their vacations and their lifestyle. And do you know what happens when you compare yourself with others and are jealous?

It is just like **"breaking our own shelter after seeing someone else house."**

And knowingly or unknowingly it is part of our daily life. But it works like a slow poison in our relationship, health, career and other areas of life. When we compare our family life with others, with people around us, most of the time we feel a little lack of feeling for ourselves. And instead of creating some good examples from them, we feel jealous of them. Which creates more situations in our life for feeling lack. Yes, it is true. I will share with you how to overcome this, but first, let me share where and how we are doing such things knowingly or unknowingly.

1. First, a very important and crucial comparison from my perspective is kids' comparison. We are so used to it. Starting with how to grow up our child? Every child needs different care. Different atmosphere. Please give them the treatment which they want as your family member.

2. Child schooling. Make your personal opinion for your child for their schooling. Do not try to show off and play with your child's future. Check their calibre also.

3. Child hobby. Please check your child's hobby and his interest in subjects. Do force every girl child for dance class and every boy for karate class. There is nothing wrong if a girl child wants to go to karate class and a boy wants to go dance class. Let them enjoy as per their interest.

4. For couples, avoid comparing your spouse with other couples. Give appreciation to each other for what they are doing right now and what they are doing for you and your family.

5. Every person is born and brought up in a different environment. So their food and nutrition value for daily life is also different. So do not compare your eating habits with others and try to shape up your body like others. Also, give freedom to people around you to choose their diet themselves. Because they know very well what their daily needs are according to their daily activity.

6. Do not compare your working hours, work liabilities, working efficiency, your job designation, your income, or your wealth with others. Every person comes from different family background. Some people choose their profession depending on situations or circumstances around them and some people choose it by their selves. By being jealous of other's professions or income you are not giving enough value to your profession or income. And because of this, there is a high chance that you might be feeling more struggle in your career. Instead of this, you can give them an appreciation for their career. By doing this, you are creating more space for good opportunities in your life to grow.

What will change?

Initially, it may be difficult for you. But once you used to give appreciation to people around you, that will become very natural for you. You started giving reason to people around you from deep inside your heart. After practising this for some days or months, you will start noticing that now you are free from any kind of jealousy. And when you start being happy in others' celebrations, the universe will give you more reasons to celebrate. And believe me, this is the most powerful exercise which I learned in my life.

Nowadays social media is a big platform to give reasons to be jealous and do comparison our self with others. So stop using social media. Yes, you read right. Stop using social media. Stop seeing post which is bothering you.

I stopped using FB and Insta around one and a half years. Also, I was feeling so much depression by reading Covid news back to back on social media. So I decided to stop opening such kinds of applications on my phone. Initially, it was not easy for me also. But now I am in the stage where I am just enjoying reading different posts of people. Even now it is part of my daily routine to appreciate at least 3 people in the morning and make them smile. And during this, I also feel so much love for them and feel blessed the whole day for myself.

Try this exercise. By doing this you are not giving reason to others' smiles, but also you feel so much light inside. You started gaining good relationships with people around you. Eventually, appreciation will become your daily routine from comparison and jealousy. I am not talking about fake appreciation or smiling toward people around you. It should be genuine.

If you are beautiful, it's God's gift to you,

If your life is beautiful then it's your gift to God.

Hope you got my point. Now begin with one more very important exercise, which also might be a little crucial for you but as important as we want to grow our life.

Forgiveness/ Let go

"I know some people are thinking to avoid this topic because it is the most emotional and hard part to forgive people who bother you, situations which you think are responsible for your present life. And you are telling me in your mind "I cannot forget my past or I cannot forgive people who have hurt me in the past. Also trying to tell me that, you don't know about my past, I have seen or experienced so many things in my past or I have gone through many things in my past etc.""

But I learnt one thing that, "Past does not exist".

And which help me to move on in my life and create new opportunities for growth and success in my personal and professional life.

By holding our past too tightly, we pull back ourselves in our life. By not letting go of your past you still cultivate old things and overthink them which lead to your relationship issues, health issues, and financial issues it destroys your life day by day for no reason.

Sometimes when you criticize someone for his behaviour for so many years and you avoid meeting such

a person in social gatherings, the other person won't have any idea about your withhold emotions because he already moved on from his behaviour. And he is enjoying his life but you are still in that emotional hurting zone and so many times you avoid some social gathering because of that person.

Which is apart from you as a socially selective person, not that person. Accept one thing, whatever you are today is just because of your creations. Somewhere you are the person who attracts all the things in your life and you are the only person who is responsible for your present situations. I know it is so way beyond hard to accept it for you. And somewhere you are criticizing me.

"Seat in a quiet place and think about it. Now you will say "how am I responsible for my situation? And even if so, how can I let go of it?"

See, what happens is, when we grew up, during that time so many things take place in our surroundings and subconsciously we grasped all things in our mind, which is reflected in our present situations. And we are unaware of it. Also sometimes we blame to universe or GOD or Jesus for putting us in that particular situation. And we forget that these all are a reflection of our own subconscious beliefs or memory.

For example, if you face loss in your business, you are frequently changing your business, or you are in so many things or business together but yet not satisfied fully and you are still searching for stability in your business. Some people invest half of their life in searching for the perfect business for them.

"Why have these things happened even though you are giving your 100% in your business? Now forget about all these things for a while and answer my questions. Is there anyone in your family member were doing this business that you are running? Is your business is given to you in legacy?"

There must be a blueprint in your subconscious mind because of that only you are getting failures in your business. I read this thing in T. Harv Aker's book "Secret of the millionaire mind".

When I read this book I connect with so many things in my life not only related to money but in relations and career points of view also.

"So the question is what is the solution for coming out with such negative blueprints and creating new positive blueprints?"

The answer is

- Healing
- Forgiveness and
- Letting go.

In today's world, it is a wildly accepted concept. Everyone knows that healing works. But the only thing is different people use a different kind of healing. To let go of your past bad memory you can do mantra chanting, Reiki healing, distance healing, Ho'Oponopono healing etc.

I used mantra chanting and Ho'Oponopono healing. Ho'Oponopono is a magical Hawaiian healing prayer. It is a technique for clearing negativity from your past memory very easily. It is a very simple yet profound technique to clear your negative thoughts and beliefs. It also clears blockages from our mind body and soul which we carried out with us since so many births. As you started clearing negativity from your path, your pathway of life will become very smooth. You can see so many opportunities in front of you, which you waiting for a long. By this prayer you can heal your health, relationship, career or money, any area of your life. To know more about this Ho'Oponopono healing prayer, you can go and join my Youtube channel "Mighty Miracle" where I have given a detailed explanation of this Prayer. If you want to join my paid sessions for 21 days, then go to the description box for more details. With this technique, you can let go of your past easily and effortlessly.

I heard somewhere that, "We have to let go of good things to achieve great things in our life, but because we are so attached to good things in our life that we might lose opportunities for great things."

CHAPTER FOUR

Change the way of talking and thinking

"Generally, we learn this only when we are going for an interview. The way of talking and thinking is coming from our outer world, our past experiences, our family background, and our knowledge about things, situations and people. So why it is important to change? What make difference in our life by changing it? And how we can change them? I am going to answer all of these questions and I hope by the end of this topic you will be ready to do it."

A normal human mind is used to thinking about negative perspectives so easily in any of the situations in our daily life.

let's take one example, now assume there is one glass of water in front of you. And I am pouring some water into it. Now let me ask one question. How much water is in the glass? Some of you can answer it by saying that half the glass is filled with water and some of you can answer that half glass is empty, right? By the way, both answers are right. No one is wrong. The only difference is the way to see the glass. Now let me add one more element to this. If the water inside the glass is dirty then how much water do you have to add to this glass to make this water drinking water? The answer is you need to add 10x more water or still you cannot have this water. You will just discard this water and then fill the glass with another fresh water to make it drinking water, right?

Same way when we change to see people us and situations around us, our whole thinking pattern starts getting change. We just need to develop a new positive way of thinking. Start meeting people around you without any prejudgment. Try to let go of your experience. That may happen because of our own attraction. Start taking responsibility for your own life and circumstances. You may read this line again and again in this whole book because somehow only we are responsible for our own life.

Stop blaming your parents, your past, your present, your situations, your health, the people around you, things around you everything. When you start accepting your life the way it is, you might stop complaining. Your overthinking about people and situations will be cured gradually.

How we can think positively and talk positively? Let me share about this,

1. 1. Try to wake up in the morning with a smile on your face even though you become late for the office. You can

say that "It is ok to be late sometime, or I will be reached on time".

2. If you find difficulty doing any task, you can say "everything is easy for me."

3. When you fall ill, you can say "My body is healing right now"

4. Whenever something happened around you, instead of thinking negatively first, train your brain to think positively about things.

5. Instead of telling "I am going" you can say "I will be back in some time".

6. Instead of saying "I have to do my household work myself only". Say "I am enjoying my household work.

When you remove words that create some disturbance in your routine life, your life will be becoming smooth day by day.

I used to say "No news is good news."

Because of this sentence, even though I will not get any opportunities to talk with my near and dears, I never get disturbed. Because subconsciously this sentence is printed very nicely in my mind. And I know if I am not getting in touch with them, they are perfectly fine. And this is how I could focus on my work without any distractions.

Similarly, instead of talking about past bad memory, or any negative situation or gossiping about someone, start to talk about things that you want to attract in your life. As I told you in the previous chapter "past doesn't exist." Stop talking about memory. Concentrate on the things which you want in your life. I am sure you all have seen the "small Buddha monk statues" set of 4 very popular now a day for home decor. What do they want to say? They just want to spread the message that

- Do not speak wrong.
- Do not see wrong.
- Do not hear wrong.
- And Do not think wrong.

If you follow these 4 simple rules about thinking and talking more than 50% of issues of daily life will resolve soon.

Now you can make a list of the sentences which you think to be changed. And you will start noticing changes in your life after some time.

CHAPTER FIVE

Creation of New Belief system

"A belief system that comes with you from your childhood. Try to break your old belief to generate new positive beliefs in your life. Sometimes it is quite difficult for you, so you can use a different kind of innovative ideas for your constant focus on your thoughts that irritates you."

You can write down all the positive aspects which you want to build in yourself on some sticky notes and stick them on a wall where you spend more time. A home engineer can paste it on your kitchen wall.

Others can place in your workplace. You can write it down in your Notepad or Mobile. You can put a reminder for this on every alternative hour, so you can constantly keep watch on your thinking patterns.

Be a child to create new belief system

"It is not so easy to change 20-30-40-year-old belief breaks in one go. So do not bother or pressurize yourself. Be easy with yourself and give some time to yourself as a small child. As we always give enough time to small kids to do their daily job by themselves after some certain age or their convenience, which is different for every child. In the same way, we should give ourselves enough time to accept new positive beliefs. Instead of beating ourselves by saying, it is always impossible for me or I cannot do it or I am not good enough to do such work, give patience to yourself to accept a new belief or used to it."

How did my belief work for me?

I have had one strong belief in my mind since the early age of my childhood that is "Rich people are having a good pure heart. They are very humble and kind nature". See this is my personal view, and also there is nothing negative in this belief.

It is very important which kind of belief you are carrying with you for a long. Is it impact in your life positively or negatively? Because of my belief in Rich people, I always feel comfortable with economically good people. I connect with such people very easily. I never hesitate to connect with them. Actually, I feel more comfortable when I am with such people. Why I gave this Rich people example that you will get to know later in this book.

Self Sabotage

At the same place, some people are hesitating to talk with financially good people. They avoid such people in social gatherings and meetings. They think that, how can I talk to them? They are some extraordinary people; I don't have such calibre or education to talk with them etc.

Actually, this is our view to see others. This sentence you will find so many times in your reading journey of my book.

We are the only person who stops ourselves to take the first step because of our old belief. This belief comes into your life from people around you, your experience, or circumstances around you. But it is most important how you take it in your personal experience.

So try to be open to any kind of opportunities in your life instead and create a new belief for yourself that is good for you and which uplift your life into better version of you.

CHAPTER SIX

Everyday Actions / Passion

"Finding your true passion and living life fully for your passion is a very important key to living a happy life. Because when you find your true passion, you will literally feel joy during fulfilling it. It will not give you much stress or burden for completing."

HOBBY

Find your hobby. We saw that in Covid time people enjoyed their hobbies fully. Some of you change your profession. Some of you stated working at home only. Some of you learn backing, cooking, painting, music, piano or any other musical instrument, some teachers have started their courses online and after feeling comfortable with this technology, they permanently stop offline courses, and some of you started YouTube channels. The list is unlimited right?

I enjoyed Covid time so much. I made so many DIYs during Covid time. I learn and cook so many different recipes which avoid before due to time schedules. I learn sewing, which is my dream hobby for so long. I get more

than enough time for meditation during this time. I can say Covid time is one kind of blessing for me. I can find out my true passion during this time only.

See, when you select your passion from your hobby, it will never feel like a burden to you. And when your work is from your list of hobbies, you will start enjoying it so much. You do not need any kind of motivation or push to do it properly.

> *"As we discussed in previous chapters, when you start Meditation, your inner calling is stronger. You will start to see a more clear picture of your desire. And when you do forgiveness, your path towards your desired goal or life will be smooth and effortless. So your action will not bother you. Also, your small action gives you bigger results."*

Common Mistakes

Don't try to jump out into some profession or business by watching the success of others. Most of us do that thing only. Even we encourage our children to do so. By watching other successful people, we assume that their profession is very good, They are earning so well effortlessly, so why not me or my child should follow them? And suddenly become "Lazy to Crazy". And doing such things when they suddenly come out of their comfort zone, they started feeling frustrated, annoyed, tired, irritated etc. and end up with give up.

So do not compare your profession or daily routine with others as we discussed earlier. Make your personal choice.

Small changes create big results

Start taking baby steps. Come out of your comfort zone wisely. Be generous with yourself. Give some time to yourself to adjust to new beginnings. You will notice the change in yourself and you will start to enjoy your work. And when your upgrade your career you will feel proud of yourself that you are taking consistent action. By doing this you will fall in love with your work and goal.

Once you start enjoying your work, no matter in which situation you are. No matter where you are? You will surely enjoy your work. And once you love what you doing no one can stop you. No one can pull you down.

Remember, as I said earlier, only you are responsible for not taking action. Only you are responsible for your past, present and future.

So stop making excuses for not taking action. instead of that you can give challenges to yourself that

"I will do my best consistently to achieve my goal"

Repeat this affirmation as much as u comfortable

"I am an amazing action taker to achieve my goal."

After being ready to take action physically and mentally start making a to-do list. This is as important as your action part. Without this, there are high chances of your distraction. Start making notes of your daily tasks.

When you divided your long-term goal into small parts of a short-term goal, a monthly goal, a weekly goal, and then a daily goal, it is so easy for you to reach your desired destination.

Self-care and Self-awareness

"This is one of the most important tools to upgrade your life to the next level. If you understand this properly you might learn how to make 360-degree changes in your life gradually."

Now you might be wondering how is it possible. Because I always brush my teeth. I am taking bath regularly. I comb my hair regularly; I am taking care of myself daily. Still, there is no remarkable change in my life. What are you talking about Jalpa? Ha ha... I am talking about a much deeper level.

I am talking about emotional, mental, and physical care of ourselves. Which is way beyond important than brushing your teeth, taking bath or combing your hair regularly.

The first tool is Meditation. We already discussed deeply in the previous chapter how meditation helps us in our routine life and how meditation changes my life also. So I am not going to get you into this topic again. I just want to remind you that by your inner child calling you can easily find your need. Whether it is fam, glam, success, relationship, care, motivation etc. the list goes on and on beyond your imagination.

The thing is that we don't time for ourselves. Most of the time we keep busy with non-productive things rather than producing one. Which we realize later on when we are already left with so much time.

Because time doesn't stop for us.

for example, when you seat to do online shopping for a mixer grinder, even though you already decided that you will go with a Philips mixer, you started searching for more of them also. After spending around half an hour you get back to your decision that the Philips mixer is best and let's buy that one. During this whole process, you do not even realize that you have already gone through more than half an hour only searching for a mixer grinder that is already conformed to buy. I was also a victim of such a situation in the past till I realize that where my time shorts? This kind of thing happened more with women than men. Women have more habits of doing comparisons or experimenting with all things and ended up only choosing one or nothing.

By the way, men have also their own way where they do not realize the time limit. For example, watching V, gaming, or spending time with electronic devices.

> "*This is just an example. We spend so much on such kind of non-productive activities and then complain that 'I don't get time for myself'. Remember every human being has the same time in one day 24 hrs a day. How some people are growing in their life so fast, easily and effortlessly and some*

*people are busy to complaining about short of time.
Think about it.* **"**

Start prioritizing your work. Focus on your goal. Add value to the things only which are more important to you. Which will help you to upgrade your life.

See having any hobby or doing some creative work is not a bad idea. Some entertainment is a must in our life. But how is it when your hobby or interesting work becomes your passion and later on turns into your earning source? We will discuss this thing in the next chapter but for now, my main intense is to let you know that rather than wasting such time, you can invest this time in your care and personal growth.

Pampering yourself is as equally important because while you pamper yourself you feel more relaxed, calm and different from yourself. You started loving yourself.

When you love yourself, you do not need anyone from outside to love you. Eventually, you feel that your complaints about seeking importance from others will disappear.

And you notice that, even though you do not need anyone to love you, respect you, or listen to you, people around you started loving you, respecting you, and listening to you. People started giving you so much importance which you complaining about for so long. Things will change automatically.

It is called **self-love.**

Self-love is not finished here only by pampering yourself. It has a very huge meaning but pampering ourselves is one of them.

The second very important thing is 'How much are you aware of our physical and mental health?

Health should be a primary goal. As we all know that "Health is Wealth". We human being forget about health while running behind wealth.

> *"I remember, I read somewhere in an article in which our honourable industrialist Mr Ratan Tata gave some tips to young youth about success and growth in our life, where he suggests that do not forget to focus on your health while you are busy to achieving your goals. Because on this journey a very fine day you may achieve everything you want, a beautiful house including all luxury, the best dream car, big business, financial freedom everything but what would you do with all of these things when you don't have good health to enjoy these luxuries?"*

He said that; I always regret about this thing that nobody was there in our time to teach us all these things and we run behind to get success and growth. But forgotten about health. So please consider your health as a priority.

So develop some good habits which upgrade your physical and mental health. Nowadays every person knows very well, what are good habits. But we procrastinate for such things by giving so many reasons about time, situations and people around us.

Hey, tell me "will you give any reason for not taking part in KBC if you get a chance to seat in front of Mr Amitabh Bachchan?"

If your answer is "I will go to meet Mr Bachchan anyhow" then let me remind you, it is not as easy or a one-day process to go and wind up with a one-hour shooting. It takes a whole day and leads to more days which takes so much time from your busy schedule. But I know, you will easily manage and prioritize things to accomplish your mission to meet Mr Bachchan. Some of us are even ready by saying this "It is worth meeting Mr Bachchan even if they do not win any prize". Am I right?

So here is my point of view to let you know that if we can give that much value to other people then why we can't get 15-20 min daily for that person – you- yourself who is much more important to you in this whole universe. Without him nothing is matter.

So please keep some time aside for yourself, especially for some physical activity. It could be anything like walking, cycling, any sports you like, yoga whatever you enjoy most.

Benefits of doing regular exercise:

1. It improves your ability to do routine activities.
2. It maintains your blood sugar level.
3. It builds up good muscles.
4. It gives strength to you in building muscles.
5. It reduced the risk factor of your psychosomatic disease.
6. It manages your weight.
7. It improves your brain functions and memory power.
8. It gives strength to your bones ad the main thing is you become more physically active.

And when you become physically more active, absolutely you will grow towards your goal setting.

So please start investing at least 15-20 min every day for the most important person in your life that is "YOU". Right now make a reminder on your phone for the first few days so you will easily remember it. Later on, it will be part of your life automatically when you feel immense changes in yourselves.

Some evolving tips

"Initially, it was really difficult for me also to bring some time for myself, but once I decided to accept good changes in my life to enhance a better version of myself I learn to keep aside "ME" time for myself. I started awake early morning before my husband and my daughter was awake. Because I understood that it is much more important to bring out some time for my own care if I want to give a better life to my family and my household activities. I started waking up at 6 AM instead of 7 AM, then 5:30 AM, then 5:00 AM and right now for more than one and half years, I used to wake up in the morning around 4:15 AM to 4:30 AM, which keeps me full of energy the whole day."

Even though I used to wake up so early in the morning, I start my household work after 8 o'clock only. Till that whole 3 hrs. are dedicated for me only.

I used to put my phone on aeroplane mode from 10 PM to morning 8 o'clock. So my mind will not distract by any kind of social media messages or any other things. I used to do meditation, OM chanting, mantra chanting, yoga, some stretching exercise, my Graphotherapy, writing my gratitude journal and things I like to do for myself which keep me so much active throughout the day.

And believe me, all these small activities have had a huge impact on my life. My life is transformed drastically physically and mentally.

So do not wait for anybody to push you, only you can push yourself for a better version of yourself.

Knowledge

"Getting knowledge in a particular field is a key ingredient action part to upgrading our life towards success. Getting knowledge and Learning new skills keeps you active forever. In this modern age, we are facing challenges in spite of having good degrees or scores in education. So here I want to share with you that rather than only collecting degrees, take knowledge in that field which you enjoy most to do work."

Louise Hay gave herself a ballroom dance class as a gift on mid of her 70s. She wants to learn dance since her childhood but she could not get a chance or she might be afraid before. Finally, she motivates herself to do what she wanted to do for a long.

Age is just a number. It is not a barrier to learning.

There is no age limit or any criteria to learn something new. It keeps you motivated and young when you focus to learn something new, your brain keeps busy thinking about those new things only, which matter to your skills.

you automatically distract from outside world situations which are bothering you. Your focusing ability

will increase. Also when you enjoy something which you like to do, your work efficiency will automatically increase. No one has to push you to complete your task. When you complete a task yourself, you start celebrating your success and you motivate to keep continue doing such things.

So from now onwards you do not need any motivation from the outside world for your growth.

Create your own world

Whether it is a small or big size of success, it doesn't matter. Your satisfaction and happiness matter. Do you know there is a special hormone released when you celebrate your success, called dopamine which played an important role in your brain and motivates you more to learn things that keep you happy. Learning new things is not only for retired people or school-going students or players or artists. It applies to every human being. Now the home engineer will ask me, is it possible for us also? How can we learn something new only sitting at home or doing only household Work?

"*By the way, I can write a book on this topic what women can do by sitting at home only. But for now, I would like to share some ideas only. A house engineer who loves to cook can learn new recipes and post them on social media and can start an online channel. They can teach other people offline or online how to do cooking. By sharing their ideas can teach different online courses. They can learn baking and start a baking business from home only. No need to go outside. Do you know baking is the*

most powerful tool to heal anxiety and depression,
proven in studies of Psychology?"

These are some examples only. The topic is beyond your imagination. So let's not get into deep so much. Now coming back to the Gentlemen.

Otherwise, they will say I don't give any idea for them. There are so many things men can do also, or learn in their professional life. After COVID Most of the world is being digital. There is a huge demand for digital expertise in the market. You can share your expertise on your social media to aware people around you and it will easy for them to connect with you. The market is overloaded with online courses. You are just away with one simple click.

Passion and Profession

Find your passion and start learning with parallel your profession. why learning more things apart from our study and profession is important? See, we are all aware of Covid situations. People with different skills easily survived. Now let me discuss the most important topic of every human being's life. That is wealth and money. By learning new things or multiple things, you have a large market to grow financially. You will never feel short of money. Whatever the financial situation, you have confidence in yourself that can come out from this easily. Also learning different skills keeps you motivated to earn money by doing different businesses.

I create my world

Let me share my example here. After being a certified pharmacist, I did medical transcription course, thinking about settling down in America. Somehow it was not possible. So I started doing a job as a pharmacist in a private firm, then the government. After leaving a government job, again I started doing a job in a private firm as a pharmacist. During this time started doing network marketing business. Also did a job as a medical transcriptionist.

If I did not have that transcriptionist experience, then I might be not able to type my book so fast on my laptop. I have very good typing speed like steno.

Learning something or getting knowledge about something, never becomes useless. These are all things done within 10 years.

after marriage did a job in a call centre for a few months only. which also I left in a few months because of my pregnancy. After delivery, I decided to do something again and focus on things that I like to do. So I did work as a Mahendi artist, which is just part of my hobby. also did baking business from home only. But believe me, this craving for learning brings me today as an "Author" to inspire you guys.

I never thought a single time that being a pharmacist How can I do a job in a call centre or how can I do work as a Mahendi artist? instead of this I always got great respect from people.

Knowledge craving

So I want to say that, learning something or gaining knowledge is never a waste. Somehow in some way, it is always useful to us in our lifetime. Also, I'm not stopping myself here only during COVID. I started learning to heal and then started healing others also as a certified healer. Then I learn Handwriting analysis, Graphology, the law of attraction and things that are much more automatically coming my way. I think there are no limitations to learning. Keep learning new things gives you more reasons to stay active and fit. Still, I'm always curious to learn many more different courses which are helpful for me and the people around me. So I can add much more value to others' lives and help them to live a happy life.

Life changing experience

Let me share about my recent achievement as a Graphologist. I get an international platform to add value to other's lives as a certified graphologist. With handwriting analysis, I can rectify the writer's character, personality, behaviour and health issues. This science has blown away my mind when I got tremendous health changes in myself using it, which I never thought to happen with scoliosis disability. Also, people who are practising it with me are getting amazing results with this. So keep taking knowledge. You may not know where your destiny is.

CHAPTER NINE

Be comfortable with change

"When you start following the above steps, your life starts to be changed positively. You might be feeling a little different in the initial stage, but do not stop here only."

Just go with the flow.

You must start enjoying your life.

By accepting new positive changes, ordinary people may start judging you. They might be talking about you. Because now you have learned different thinking and talking pattern, they might feel uncomfortable with you. Because now you do not have any interest in gossiping about anyone. Or now you do not want to discuss your problems. Ordinary people may think that you become arrogant, but it is ok. Stay with your new nature of forgiveness. Let go of all unwanted people and situations around you.

As I said before now you started attracting people and situations according to your likes and dislikes. Maybe some of your family members or some of your good friends get left behind. I mean to say, it may happen that friends with whom you discussed your problems for long hrs, suddenly they stop reaching out to you. And you wondered, how is it possible that for long we didn't even talk! But don't worry, it is just a process. When you start vibrating at a certain frequency, you only attract people around you matching with your frequency.

You suddenly start feeling a new environment around you, filled with new positive people. Who is interested in growth? Their primary language is appreciation. They are already successful or on a path to success. They understand you, help you and motivate you 24x7. You find them energetic 24x7. They are very much positive about all prospects of life.

I am somehow already blessed since long having amazing friends in my life. Who always motivated me, and appreciated me and my work. I have learned so many skills by having lots hobby, they never judge me or rises any questions about my skill. They always gave me the right world for me without any partiality. I always tell them about the pillar of my life. Hold such people in your life forever.

Learn to say "NO"

Learn to say "NO" that people who used to take benefit from you. It may be about asking for some help financially physically or emotionally. Every time giving them chance to take advantage of you and feeling guilty is an injustice to yourself. By telling them the truth you can be free from any kind of dishonesty.

By doing this you can be feeling much more relief and be able to focus on your work. Politely being clear with your decision can make feel relaxed.

Now when you come out from unwanted situations and people around you, you will find enough time to create something new in your life. Try to follow your daily tasks by making time table, so you get to know how much time you have for your daily routine, and extra how much value you can add day to day to upgrade yourself.

The power to say "NO" will give you all miseries of your life. What if everyone is happy around you only you are not? Think about it.

CHAPTER TEN

Financial changes

"I am sure, you will agree with me that managing money is a very important part for keep our daily life stress free. People having more than good enough financial conditions have faced stress to manage money in their life. How to save tax, where to invest money and some others like these. People having lack money in their life have another kind of stress like how to make more money. And there is a third category also, where people having good enough money to survive, never feel a lack of money situation but still face stress about money, just by constantly overthinking their future financial situation. And because of this, you might be not able to enjoy your present situation. Yes, now a days major part of us facing this situation. Yes, now give poise yourself and think about it for a sec. R you among them? Maybe or may not. But yes, I was among them."

When I took small baby steps in my life, which I have discussed in previous chapters, I started enjoying my life. I stopped myself to get into an unusual discussion about money. And when I stop false discussions about money with my husband and the people around me, I felt like I am wealthy enough. And I could see money coming into my life from unexpected sources.

I started being grateful for my financial condition. And believe me, when money will be not an issue in your daily life, you feel like more than 70% of life is perfectly going well.

> *"When I read T. Harv Eker's "Secret of the Millionaire Mind", Napoleon Hill's "Think and Grow Rich", and "Rich Dad Poor Dad", I started thinking differently. I changed my perspective on money. Which become helpful to me in upgrading my life to the next level. The very common thing in these books, which I noticed is they insist to change our old beliefs about money. "*

If you want to be a millionaire then follow millionaire people's habits. Think like a millionaire. Accept changes on your way to millionaire. You cannot be a millionaire with your past beliefs or experience about money. I could relate to T. Harv's money blueprint story.

I learned from Dr. John Demartini's teaching, a very powerful tool to stay happy or stress-free is Delegation. By delegating things, you can focus more on the work which you like to do. And you can be more productive. By applying this tool you can actually improve your financial condition. To know more about this deeply, you can go through Dr. John Demartini's YouTube videos.

I also interrupt my old money-making patterns and beliefs, Like

1. We can earn money through hard work only.
2. Asking for money from someone is bad.
3. Debts are not good for financial security.
4. One should secure their future by buying a house or investing in the property only.
5. Only money and wealth can make me happy.

Now let's move on to the next chapter one of my favourite daily practice "Gratitude."

CHAPTER ELEVEN

Gratitude

"Gratitude is the most powerful technique among all techniques which I am going to share with you. You might have a question, why do I put it in the last? Let me give you an answer. Because I want you to remember this technique 24x7 and start this practice as you finish this last chapter. For the last two years, my day start with gratitude and ends with gratitude practice only. Why gratitude is important in our daily life? How we can practice it? Let's discuss it."

Turning point

Life turned out when I started reading Rhonda Byrne's book **"The Magic"**. The whole book is based on gratitude practice only which covered almost all areas of our life. How we can be grateful for our past bad experiences, people whom we can't accept in our life, situations which we don't want in our lives and many more things. Especially feeling gratitude about negative situations and people, how makes difference in our life, that just blew away my mind.

I also started exercising all her teaching from this book. And believe me, I can feel changes in my life. Day by day I learned very nicely about this practice and I started writing a "Gratitude journal".

Gratitude journal writing

There are three ways to write a gratitude journal. You can say this technique scripting also. You can be grateful for your past good or bad memories. You can be grateful for your present situation. And third, you can be grateful in advance for things you want in your future.

Now, many times people ask me how I start to write a journal. Which would be the first thing? And my answer to the foam of questions is "Are you Alive?", "Are you awake today morning and able to see this beautiful world?" and the answer I receive most probably is "Yes". Then I suggest being grateful for that. Many people in the world sleep at night and couldn't wake up in the morning. They don't get opportunities to see the next day's sunlight due to heart attacks in the sleep. So you should be grateful to that Universe/ God/ Allah/ Jesus/ Divine power whatever you called him every day. The more you become grateful you will attract more reasons in your life to be grateful.

You can change your emotions through this practice also. If you feel uncomfortable with any situation in your life, start being grateful for others' part of that situation and you will see the situation being comfortable to you slowly and gradually.

I read Robin Sharma's quote "Everything is created twice, first in the mind and then in reality." So we should choose our thought very carefully. Try to be aware of your thoughts. How to create new thoughts by affirmation,

Let me put some examples from my scripting technique

1. I am grateful for another beautiful morning I can see with my eyes.
2. I am grateful for having food daily easily.
3. Thank you universe for my healthy and joyful family.
4. Thank you universe for my beautiful home.
5. I am grateful for my mobile.
6. I am grateful for all the money which spent till today on my education.
7. I am grateful for this oxygen I breathe free of cost.

The list is unlimited. Because we never thought of all these things we are using without even asking for them. The universe gives us FREE, and still, we are mostly living in complaining mode.

As you wake up in the morning, say thank you to the Universe. And when you go to the bed, say thank you for all the small things which you got today without asking for them.

Start this practice right now and you will notice how things will change around you. You will start noticing miracles in your life. Maybe initially you will find some difficulties to say "Thank you" to your problems or people who bother you but with continue practising it daily, you will find situations under control now.

Start enjoying a new life. It is never too late to make things right.

Conclusion

"Feeling motivated? Maybe you are thinking that all things together are not possible for you. Maybe you think will it make any difference in your situation or challenge you are facing right now. If there is no change in your life for a long then try at least any of these tools for a few days just for a change. Do not let the fear your unknown boss. Only you can take action for yourself."

Do not think too much about others. I am not telling you to be selfish. Remember your main intention to be happy is to make happy others. You can feed others only when you have food to feed. We can contribute things only that we have in abundance.

Start to plan your day according to your routine.

1. Get at least 5 to 10 min a day for meditation.
2. Let go of your past. Forgive the people who hurt you the most. Send them lots of blessings every day.
3. Start taking care of yourselves. Give yourself rewards for the good actions you make daily.
4. Spend your free time on your hobby or things you like to do most.
5. Be the voice of yourselves. Learn to say "NO".
6. Create new beliefs which are good for you.
7. Do not hesitate to change your thinking and talking patterns.
8. Accept the changes to create a new world of happiness around you. Avoid unnecessary arguments and negative

people around you.

9. Manage your finance and create new beliefs for Money.
10. Try to stay 24x7 in gratitude. Smile is the priceless ornament we can carry throughout the day.
11. Do not give your emotions remote control in others' hands. Do not allow people around you to deplete your energy.

Start work on these basics and see how life turns 360 degrees.

Do you know why the Bamboo plant is so much precious? It takes a long time to come out from the soil in comparison to other plants or trees. But during this time roots of bamboo expand so strongly that even high winds cannot damage it or it is never shaken by any climate changes once it comes out from the soil. It is the most precious grass in terms of its usage.

Same way, it is not important how much time you take to learn constantly light and happy in any situation in your journey of life. More important is, to come out as strong as a bamboo tree so that from now onwards any cyclone cannot destroy your life.

Acknowledgements

I am grateful to the Almighty for giving me this opportunity to add value to the society around me. Thank you, God for giving me enough strength, inspiration, intelligence, spectacular health, a blissful mind and endless passion.

Next, I would like to give huge credit to my school teachers and college professors for their constant guidance, supervision and hand-holding teachings. Some of them are showering their blessings on me from heaven right now. I am lucky to work with many great people during my professional career who always being kind-hearted, caring, and supportive throughout my professional journey. I really appreciate it.

Special thanks to my mentors Mitesh sir- Indu mam and Imran sir for their continuous support, encouragement and guidance. Thank you for making my life flawless. I would like to thank my magician friends from the recent community who also walking on a path to adding value to the society along with me. Thank you for being one of the best and most encouraging colleagues.

Next, I would like to thank all people and situations created around me because of that I am able to make this content. I am grateful for all people who help me knowingly or unknowingly with their suggestions, support and timely help to make this content possible.

A big thanks to my family members. My source of creation, my parents, who taught me the importance of moral values and humanity in my life. I am grateful for their constant support and trust in my craving for learning. I am grateful to my husband for supporting me and encouraging me to start a new venture in my life. feeling blessed to have three sparkling stars of my family, my daughter Parishri and nephews Vihaan and Sarvam who always being there to teach new-age lessons with fun and creativity. I am really grateful to my extended family members for their constant support and trust in me.

Last but not least, a big Thank You to YOU for selecting this book and taking action for yourself to "Be like a Butterfly".

Please remember to write to me about how this book helped you. Please leave your feedback after reading this book on Amazon. It will encourage others and inspire them to take action to upgrade their life.

Love you,
Jolly Jalpa.
Healerjalpa.22@gmail.com
Penphysio22@gmail.com